Edgemere

Poems

Steven Riel

LILY POETRY REVIEW BOOKS

Published by Lily Poetry Review Books
223 Winter Street
Whitman, MA 02382

https://lilypoetryreview.blog/

ISBN: 978-1-7365990-5-1

Cover design: Martha McCollough

Cover Photo: "Edgemere Drive-In, Shrewsbury, MA," Len Arzoomanian

Contents

I.

In this world (of which I am the author) I am not the only denizen, citizen, harlequin, or doyenne. I have invented myself, surely, who hasn't, but I unlike (perhaps) you, have invented others—assorted godlettes, hopefuls, poseurs, and freaks.

—Katie Farris

SAND PILE WITH SISSY

I was not drawn to haul dirt
in a Tonka truck, to grade the damp
sand of lanes planned to wind
through quaint suburban developments,
nor bugle with spitty lower lips
the exhales of down-shifting.

My pals battled over claw loaders,
with the vanquished carting culverts
on flatbed trucks crosstown.
I never had to tussle because
no other nearby boy coveted the chariot
I lusted for: a vermillion station wagon,
its glossy enamel brash as nail polish.

My make-believe errands proved the utility
of byways laid out by the boyish boys
& their dirty hands (though under my breath
I'd tut-tut about construction delays,
the dust they would deposit on my dashboard).

I'd take unnecessary detours I called caprices
the long way back from the butcher's
to feel the breeze flatten my chiffon scarf
while I'd dream that I drove an aerodynamic convertible
& its Forward Look—"Suddenly it's 1960!"
"Rocket ahead in glamourous style!"—
or the Lincoln Landau that full-page ads
I scrutinized on our coffee table
showed accompanied by a cocktail
dress, a rich beau to swing open
the passenger door like a well-trained dog.

Joey & John shook hands on laying a railway spur
through their sand & gravel—while I pictured
the BIG plaid, BIG threads of my car coat's
elbow-length sleeves, its implausible collar;
& reveled in my soap-opera worries:
would the bold red of this wagon in its carport
clash with the cedar-stained shakes of our ranch?
Would the watermelon carved into a baby buggy
I discovered in one of my mother's cookbooks
& oh-so-ached to fill with grapes & melon bites
earn me oooo's at my best friend's shower?

When my salt & pepper Rock
Hudson husband returned from the city
to find the workmen gone, our neighborhood
completed, & me with fresh lipstick,
puckered for a kiss, would he be pleased,

or open his eyes one dawn & see me
as a maraschino fossil
buried in last week's Jell-O mold?

SHOOT TO KILL, OR, YOU'LL
BE GLAD YOU USED GLADE

Since I'm a fifth-grade fag
who gets throttled in the skunk-cabbage swamp
where the teacher's aide can't see,

better to pretend I'm
the high-heeled mom in the commercial
protecting her split-level family—
the Glade Lady who shields what she can
from what reeks. Better to press with a manicured finger
a recessed plastic button as gracefully
curved as an Edsel's dashboard.
Better to target with—look—disodium phosphate
any enclosed & tight spaces
where germs or Viet Cong
cluster: diaper pails, disposals,
fringed ditches around rice fields
egg-beaten by helicopters. No place to hide.

No way to escape.
Better to say my tummy aches & stay home.
Better to wave a sweeping wand—
oh, if I had a wand like Glinda's
that would—*poof!*—change me into a spray of freesia
guaranteed by the makers of Johnson's Wax.

On TV, above the coffee klatch's bridge game,
one curlicue squirt, & stuffiness just seems to vanish.
Better not propose a science project
tracking the fate of floral-sachet molecules,
whether they sponge overcast skies. A trade secret
makes indoor air fresh as all outdoors.
Better not mail in a postcard
asking for the ingredients.

At quarter past noon, the news anchor
tallies yesterday's usual
domino death toll.
As the world turns, better to glide
with an Aqua-Netted bob
from toilet to hair trap to garbage can
in a starched, full-skirted dress.
Better not wonder what mothers ask themselves
during afternoons over irons.
Better not dwell on rice.

Instead I advance, finger poised
to make cigarette smoke & last night's
liver fumes sweet as a spring shower
thanks to a harmless chemical
that eradicates odors & frees up
an hour for girly boys
to inch into elbow-length rubber gloves
& savor the zest of miraculous
Easy-Off as it turns hard
black grease into soft brown soap
I just rinse down the drain.

INCUBATION OF A STAR

She plants her self
before a full-length Brooklyn mirror,
Noxzemas away her mother's makeup,
tests countless ploys
to coax the front row's gaze
anywhere but *Here she honks, there she blows!*
Big Beak! Big Beak!, anywhere but
arms so scrawny her *meshuggah* mama
shipped her off to health camp
for fattening at age five.
In the waist-up audition
above their bathroom vanity,
she cat-eyes eyeliner angles,
critiques collarbone and earlobes
four or five hours a day.
Cultivates the longest red fingernails
ever to read a part; favors offbeat necklines,
feathery earrings, slanted hats.
When cat calls bring out the genius
in her drag-queen pals,
she marks their technique.
Drops a letter from her forgettable forename,
practices a collection of odd gestures till they're hers,
till she debuts on Broadway
with oh what a voice and oy what a schnozz
we have to applaud.

IN MY LIDDY DOLE SWEATER

I first took Liddy out for her debut
in Houston at the Strange Door.
Entire agencies kowtow
to my fitted shoulders
when I cross the stage
in tailored herring-bone.

After shaving backwards
& forwards & sideways,
I Visine both eyes,
pulverize any mascara clumps,
screw on pearl-button earrings.

I follow her brutal routine
except she wakes up before dawn
when I'm slippering
my Size-12E bunions home,

but Tuesdays over toast
in her condo that I conjure wholesale,
I get all Big Girl Wistful
as I consider the Watergate pool.
A randy driver waits in the lobby
beside arranged hydrangeas. Suzanna,
my Girl Friday, totes my slim briefcase.

I convene board meetings at 8:59 sharp.
A squad of lesser beauty queens
has the handouts binder-clipped,
my PowerPoint queued up,
talking points bulleted.

In lipstick this tasteful, I am confident
consensus will be won,
petty interests put aside,
the City upon a Hill rise up, rain-washed,
with epidemics quashed.

I can assure you that, like snowdrop blossoms,
segregation in Salisbury just faded.
No, I never paid much mind
to tailgate jamborees.

Once I've fastened Our Senator's
modest lashes,
I feel in my knees
how hard it was
to look pretty while climbing
a ladder in pumps
past preps at Harvard.

Dressed as Liddy Dole,
I toe-heel my Tri-Delt step across fairgrounds,
nibble corn dogs without a smear,
drawl back at my constituents' drawl,
and smile a genuine smile.

IN SEARCH OF DELLA STREET

"Have you ever looked into a mirror with another mirror?"—Katie Farris

There are five characters with glaring grudges
    who'd love to gloat, wielding a bloody bookend
        astride the decedent's body,

but the mystery I aim to solve, re-run after re-run,
    is the missing woman sitting in Perry's office:
        his stenographic sidekick.

Outfitted with sharp pencil,
    blank pad, perfect cursive,
        she intercoms Gertie out in Reception,

brings in a tray with after-hours coffee,
    safely delivers a platter of sandwiches
        just past Paul Drake's boyish reach.

Hello, Beautiful, sing-songs that detective
    whenever he strides through Mason's back door,
        reminding us to notice her.

Does this confidential secretary get secret credit
    off-screen or in her paycheck
        for anticipating Perry's next move:

having water already boiling in the percolator
    to steam open an envelope? Or for slipping him
        an insight in a folded note before he cross-examines?

The only fact I can introduce after years
    of investigation is this career woman's
        attractive, admiring, alert

face glued to her employer's.
    I can produce as proof of her priorities
        her statement that the cost of a pair of torn hose

shouldn't prevent the two of them from pushing through
    thick brush to discover more clues.
        One day the scriptwriters let her show some

wit, & she greets Paul with *Hello,*
    Beautiful, before he can open his mouth.
        But when Perry teasingly asks,

in one episode's denouement,
    whom *she's* sweet on, & with a flash in her eyes,
        she replies, *You'd be the last to know,*

I blurt out, *Perry, can't you see she's guilty*
    of being schooled
        to hide her soul?

THE WOMAN WITH A TRANSPARENT PURSE

has nothing to hide.
She boards the T matter-of-factly,
in a sleeveless dress, the barest of sandals.
She's self-assured as Twiggy
in a mini at a photo shoot.
I don't need X-ray vision
to count the dimes inside
her matching change pouch,
but is this intimacy?
There's no cranny, no crevice, no cache.
She isn't ashamed of tampons, of what
Daughters of Isabella called in whispers
The Curse. I wonder if this
cellophane fashion
statement has a seam
where lint collects. She probably doesn't worry
that an accidental blow to the head
might delete her passwords.
She probably doesn't squirrel away a spare key.

Maybe she never locks her doors.
Maybe she lives in a glass house.
Imagine getting ready for work
and ready for bed
without shades, blinds, or drapes—
a mannequin?
Richly suited crowds could gawk
whenever clerks stripped us of underclothes.

Even the flashiest, swishiest goldfish
sometimes needs to hover
and rest its pucker
behind a screen of plastic plants.
Who'd choose to stand on the subway

with Lucite skin, a Visible Woman,
Fallopian tubes available
to the passing glance of every passerby?

If I had a purse, it would be the nook
where I'd tuck an assortment of worries
in the form of hot pink Pepto Bismol
and breath mints flecked with green.
Slipped among lozenges would be
daydreams and their props: a stash
of Trojans, my diaphragm,
perhaps some just-begun poems—
all membrane and heartbeat.
The last thing I'd want hanging
on two straps from my arm
would be an ultrasound of myself
advertising my jellyfish dreams.

I WAS QUITE A LOOKER

Let me put my lipstick away
and show you. Too bad
this photo's raggedy—
I've carried it in my wallet
all these years
—but wasn't I something?
I laid out a pretty penny
for that photographer on Tremont Street
when I got my diploma from Katie Gibbs.
Did those college men ever fancy me!
I could take dictation. It was easy-peasy
to land a job in the steno pool. After the war,
dance halls salt-and-peppered every ward,
and believe you me, I was no wallflower.
I jitterbugged, and I could cut a rug.
Saturday mornings, I'd shop downtown
and snap up bargains that flattered my figure.
I still have a knack for fashion—
get a load of my latest do:
Dorothy Hamill, with a little wave up front.
I admit I'm past my prime,
but doesn't my complexion keep its glow?
A lot of people notice me. Even women.
It makes me sad. Gosh, it makes me sad.

ROSEMARY WOODHOUSE

i.
In spring, once I slough off
the furry lining of my raincoat,
its shell becomes a satin sheath
billowing in breezes finally warm enough
to hold the scent of lilac.
All day as I walk, I'm Mia
Farrow as Rosemary Woodhouse
during those early weeks painted
in celadons, sleepy yellows, chicory blues—
a pastel is any hue with white mixed in,
& Rosemary devotes her days to inviting light
into a dead widow's Victorian pantry,
tacking down cheery shelf paper
in one vaguely troubling closet.

ii.
I imagine I'm you, shopping for fabric, when I'd
calmly cross Manhattan's widest avenues,
a slip of a doe-eyed, Omaha ingenue
with no money worries to fetter my gaze.
Brief, blousy dresses were the rage,
but I wouldn't keep yanking down my hem,
wouldn't fold bare arms like St. Joan's
armor across my boyish breasts.
Of course, men would leer
while my blond forearms gleamed,
but I'd float on, unruffled,
so sure I'd be
of the color scheme I'd chosen,
Guy's future as an actor,
the roulade I'd serve for dinner.

iii.
Before pain
pinched me into a clenched
stick of chalk

Before my womb became a torture
chamber, & Dr. Sapirstein stood by
while the corkscrew turned

Before the words, *Not fair to Sapirstein?*
What about what's fair to me? spouted
from the chiffon that clouded my voice

Before I wailed, *If you won't pay, then I'll p—*
& realized Guy pulled the purse strings
though I shouldered the bag

Before I found myself mirrored
in the toaster's shiny side
scarfing down raw liver
when no one was around

Before I solved the anagram
with Scrabble tiles

Before I knew that the prince who pledged
to protect me from wolves
had traded my ovum for a good part in a play

Before I gathered that like the Blessed Mother
I was a baby machine
but she had murmured, *Thy will be done,*
while they had doped me,
kidnapped my choice

Before I looked
into the eyes of Satan

iv.
Legs crossed both at ankle & knee
under her stylish kitchen chair
long after midnight,

feverish, fluorescent, she
jots on the backs of recipe cards
she'll shakily refile:

can't we still fiercely & wholly love
the fragile, first leaves of spring
though we know tent caterpillars will munch & spin

can't we sing of the pale mauve seedling's
sidelong attempt to blend in
though we know camouflage is lost on the lawnmower

can't we ache to paint a clerk's taut & creamy skin
though we've wandered nursing-home corridors
in search of a vase for cut flowers
& have witnessed what it all comes to in the end

v.
Rosemary, I want to go back
to the lullaby you lisped
while the opening credits rolled,
when Central Park was an impressionist's
serene & fragrant haze
before the camera zoomed straight down

the Dakota's facade
as though looking down an abyss,
skimming over unbeknownst to us
the window of the extra room
you'd naturally slate as
The Nursery.

        I want to go back to ask:
do we lose every shred of innocence
once we discern: that evil might smirk
in each & every corner?
That the Devil is inside us?
That whatever pastel we start out as,
life shall smudge some soot in?
That we might in fact choose the forbidden
apple, or have our judgment upended
by a baby's cry?

Was Eden a lie?

The length of my men's raincoat swish-swishes
against my summer-weight slacks.

O we were so glamorous, so poised
in our slim vulnerability

before we were forced to ask questions

—remember?

PIGEON IN SUBWAY

I followed the popcorn
constellation but
lost the sky. Maybe
the hawks, too. Far-off squeaks
talon my ears.

The grounded ones
with egret legs
crowd this shiny ledge.
Do they know the way out
but wait for crumbs?
I keep almost underfoot

and mark their moves.
No one tries to kick me. Today
they stare down—bleary-eyed
bitterns. I pity them,
their naked wings.

I bob along the yellow
edge: it's no great drop,
but reeks of rats. Biters!
Can they smell me?

A huge, squealing snake
with four red eyes
pops out of its
windy hole. I hop back
and flutter. Sideways

mouths split open the snake's side,
spitting out more herons

in a hurry. My found flock
crams inside the snake's throat,

leaving me alone to preen
while rats grind their teeth below.

A CAGE'S LAMENT

Yes, Mr. Pigglesworth, you wipe your beak
against my kiln-baked skin, but I
want to hold you—really hold you.
You know me as The Obstacle,
without understanding
that inside I become lava
whenever your feathers brush my bars.

If only I could chirrup and inform you
your incessant sawing and clawing
get you nowhere—
that I'm welded wrought iron
with recessed rivets and no exposed nuts.

It's not in my power to fall apart.
I can only hold up
your coop cup, cuttlebone,
jungle gym, and full-length mirror
so that together we can admire
the long tail of your red tuxedo. Oh.

But that strumpet Mrs. Smith
uses me to woo and ensnare you.
While she coyly calls you
Mr. Neurotic, I'm the slave hoisting her gifts
day and night: the tropical fruits, the soft-wood
toys you gnaw. If I could produce
snapshots of the former Misters she's hand-reared,
you'd cease to crave her stroking.

Even if I found a way to froth up
into gossamer netting and become an aviary,
I couldn't compete with her bottomless wallet.
While you slumbered, snug

inside my fitted night-cover,
she told her plaid nephew
she's provided for you, her final companion,
in her will. As for me,
if I'm lucky, I'm destined for a yard sale.

At least I'm always on hand to hear you
mimic the clock.
     If only I could evaporate.
At least, my pet, you take it all out on me,
instead of plucking yourself.
     If only I could rust away.
At least I winced for you
during your youthful, panicked attempts
to bite through me.
     If only I could unlatch.
At least I witness those attacks,
though they've become habit,
become halfhearted.
     If only I could speak.

INTERVIEW WITH PHYLLIS FROMME

My sister didn't do those things to hurt us.

After you called, while I sorted out my pills,
my mother's blond Danish Modern end tables
flashed through my mind.
I open the crisper, and there's Lynnie,
inside a dumpster, picking through freckled lettuce,
bent on helter skelter.
They ruined the Beatles for me.

Last night, I dreamed of a scarlet pond,
an albino koi surfacing
with the barrel of a .45
poking out of its mouth.

Yes. Father. Not well.
I took my first *full* breath the day he died.

Is it cold in here?
Father kept our thermostat low
and monitored Mother's odometer, leaving us
just quarters when he traveled for work.
I'd watch Mother and her shoulders march
her empty purse next door to scrub linoleum.

I read Lynnie said our own father
abused her (sexually I mean).
How was I supposed to know?
When he'd unlock our bedroom door,
she wouldn't hide welts that would darken, but—
the year I started kindergarten,
he stopped talking to her.
I was so young.

Redheads with spark get beaten.
I swallowed my peas.

Three years later, he spoke to Lynnie again.

I wish your editor never found me.

Did you read she took a staple gun,
aimed a line of punctures up her arm?
Ground into her skin with lit
cigarettes as if she were an ashtray?
Father told her she was ugly.
Then she met Manson.

I kept quiet, learned to sew,
traced patterns, left extra cloth.
I'd smile back at Breck girls in study hall
but couldn't invite them home,
even when Father was away.

So I'm in high school, right,
and there's Lynnie on TV,
an X carved in her brow.

I wanted my teachers to forget her.
You're the only one who remembers
she had a sister. I never corrected
teachers who said our last name wrong.
That always set Father off.
He insisted on the German way:
From-ma. From-ma.

I imagine Lynnie hunched over,
thinking, thinking, thinking in her cell.

No, I've never visited her—never will.
No, the people at work don't know.

Now I have a question for you.
Why couldn't I just have been Phyllis
Fromme, the good girl
who went to the prom?

A TIME FOR US

i.

There's a place for us—this time
the Supremes don't bounce through heartache,
bubbling to a hurdy-gurdy-with-a-skip,
one-step-away-from-a-jump-rope beat.

This time it's Ed Sullivan, 1966—an echo of
Dr. King's litany hovers above the stage.

As usual Diana, Flo, and Mary harmonize—
Peace and quiet and open air—
reminding us Whites of some city's
singed plywood we've witnessed from a train,
but tonight we hover over TV dinners
and their snugly partitioned cobbler
as Dr. King's sonorous baritone climbs this time *Somewhere.*

This is another time Motown got invited inside
paneled family rooms,
sequins flashing back at our brand-new braces
thoroughly masticating above plastic TV trays
laden with bread-plates plush with buttered Wonder-

bread. Though their mamas still scrub tile floors,
these Black girls got asked again to sing.
How unscuffed their pink pumps gleam,
V'ed along three Xs taped downstage.
With steps kept small within pink-lace sheaths,
these young ladies, properly girdled,
could never run away.

ii.

Even if *a time for us* was coming,
Flo and Mary weren't permitted to glitter
at that or any time
except as wind-up dolls, staring off
to the ceiling above the last row
as if they glimpsed *A new way of living*
where no sister hums back-up
or lowers her glued eyelashes on cue
while a diva writhes to the final held note
like a pole dancer, lost not in this perfect liberation
song's vision, but in her own
there's-a-place-for-me ecstasy.

Did bright lights bring tears
to Diana's half-closed eyes?
Six earrings like chunks of pink ice
sparkle beside shackled smiles.

II.

Oh, but a star
is no consolation for the dead.

—Andrea Cohen

Such a sleep
They sleep—the men I loved.

—Alfred Lord Tennyson

TODAY, BROTHER, YOU WOULD
HAVE TURNED 56

We *did* become cheerleaders in the end.

After high school games against Northfield,
secretly we'd stomp, clap, & pretend
we wore their squad's sado-genteel
red leather gloves. How hickster uncool!—
we'd mimic them—*slap sla-sla-sla slap*—
idolizing instead our fluffy-sweater school's
troupe, who flounced when the right rim ball dropped with a tap.

College. In this snapshot, you lifted a boulevard-wide banner's side,
shirt tied high to flaunt Coppertoned skin. Your thin gray shorts
suggested the rest. How pretty undergraduates paraded in Pride.
Head-cheerleader politico queer, I led the *hey-hey, ho-ho* retort.

No other person on Earth mocked those red leather gloves.
My thumbs drum our chants beside this photo I love.

ABEL HAS ALMOST NO IMMUNE SYSTEM

i.

The red footnote on the label of the miracle
drug catches my eye: Abel's in the 33 percent
who vomit up nearly every bite.
Mom and Dad told me he sobbed
on the long-distance call
before a catheter was tunneled
between his clavicle and first rib
so he could feed through his subclavian.
Other clinical words collide into Eden,
after pancreatitis, toxoplasmosis.
After Abel's insurance company
couldn't dropkick him fast enough.
His lover works late hours
to cover their mortgage. Wouldn't you?
I borrow shekels to board the Shuttle
to their condo. Abel lies upstairs, starving.

Just levering his bony 99 pounds
into the bathtub hurts us both.
After another 24 hours, when anyone less "gone"
would have moaned *I'm hungry,*
the feeding machine arrives:
aqua plastic box, like a vacuum cleaner;
gleaming steel caddy; plastic tubes; plastic
bags of almost fluorescent white
nourishment. Welcome to the family.

A nurse swings by to run through
instructions as intricate as life:
    1) Interlocking joints,
    2) kept sterile with alcohol wipes,
    3) spill into Abel's core.
Oh, that feels cool, he murmurs.

This mission is a booby trap,
when each step must be followed to the iota
to foil microbes. Is it possible
to be precisely prophylactic
forever and ever, and what if
someone sleepy and/or absent-minded
stumbles through what's now second shift?
How to gauge *a turn for the worse*?
I am my brother's keeper.

ii.
Yes, my name is Cain, and I'm calling about Abel.
Yes, I *do* have his patient ID.
I want to see the bill
the home-health company submitted,
the 3-D pie charts Accounting blazoned at board meetings
to extol how much moolah was pinched
by discharging failing policy-holders
into the land of Nod.

For the criminal trial, our lawyers subpoena
this quarter's financials, issue interrogatories
to establish bloated profits the LLC diversified,
how many day spas it spawned east of Eden,
how many golf courses begat
among thistle and thorn.

iii.
All evidence will be offered to Adonai.

iv.
I am the wobbly tiller in Abel's room
who paces but must keep steady.
With rigid fingers I hold the survival
of my first rival, whose birth introduced me
to the murderous scythe I swing inside.

This vigil will last days, only hours, in fact—
unto dust thou shalt return.
His sleek alarm clock sweeps silently on
while I scribble lists of specialists,
lay siege to another Help Line's moat.

Abel has no draw bridge,
one or two white cells left to rouse.
One slip, one contaminated swipe—
if only I could kneel beside his bed and believe.

ANOTHER WINTER BEGINS

The day we buried you

chilled like this morning: its brisk

wind whistling into uncovered ears;

stark sunlight unfiltered by

leaves recently felled

in storms; and a sense of less

sheltered space, now we could stare through

a fence of trees, witness how

their black twigs reach like fingertips

every which way towards light,

trunks edging row upon row of flat

granite graves, till anemic clouds

drifted in, softening nothing.

THERE WAS A CRASH

Cleaning woman drops our portrait,

        cracks glass

decades after shutter-snap.

            Back then, wren-boned, I posed

beside your newly hunky torso

        flexed beneath tuxedo,

your radiant blond wave

        (from a bottle—a brother knows),

that sun-shot noon we squared shoulders and sang *Cheese*: basking

        ushers at our sister's first no-guarantees

I do.

        How could we guess what would crash?—

one of my few framed photos of you, still intact

    despite this fracture

arcing between our bowties,

        scarring your just-shaved cheek?

How can I blame diligent Ana's

        Endust fingers

when I, too, could have held tighter,

        even if unable to sustain

T-cells patrolling your bloodstream

        on this breath-fogged side of the glass?

IT TOOK 29 YEARS TO SAY

logically I wouldn't
mumble the Mass
through the entire funeral
because by slipping into its rhythm
I'm endorsing the usual
sermon about how this is
the happiest of days.
Logically I wouldn't tell
my asshole brother-in-law
I love you before we square
our shined oxfords on the withered
turf beside the hearse, then step
towards the rectangular hole.
Logically I wouldn't
seek your healthy
face between clouds,
nor address the air.

ECHO

i.
I creep up to the postal clerk
and, with a low and quavering voice,
ask for a stamp
to Heaven. She leafs through
waxy envelopes. Four cents.
I don't hold up the line
to whisper *Can I use just any post box?*
I wonder about an unmarked
holding bay in the regional postal center,
whether our letters get launched
after midnight from some Utah desert.
Since this stamp exists—I'm pinching it—
other mourners must have used it,
but why haven't I heard? If it were advertised,
surely there'd be a stampede
at opening time.
Am I allowed to mention
the sticky-on-one-side rectangle
I've tucked inside my backpack's only
pocket within a pocket?

ii.
Of course, I don't have his address
filed under "R" in my small spiral notebook.
Anxious to avoid *Return to Sender,*
I'll include my brother's middle name,
make sure my penmanship's legible
as I loop the letters *P a u l*—
the name of the second saint
(writer of epistles)
invoked at my brother's baptism
to rudder and shield him.

iii.
Inside the purple and white stamp
I become an astronaut
on a spacewalk, surveying Earth
beyond absurdly high clouds.
The peninsula below
bears no shape I've studied on my globe.
A craterless white orb,
moon-sized (this might be
an optical illusion), hangs close by,
glowing like a pearl. Am I standing
on anything? A space ship's invisible
bridge staffed by archangels?
Evenly curved lines beam back
and forth between
this sphere and Earth's two hemispheres—
study-hall doodles of wave-like transmissions
bounced from the sunlit half of our planet
to the invisible side.
Boing. I'm floating in a cartoon,
framed by capital letters spelling out,
COMMUNICATIONS FOR PEACE, ECHO I.
                              Wait a minute—
am I untethered, untethered, untethered?
If I turn my head, will I find
a gate, a blessèd host,
my brother's open, lesion-free arms?

iv.
Where to begin?
                    Dear dearest David

Is he beyond names?
                    Are you okay?

Am I limited to one side

of a single feather-heft sheet

of powder-blue onion-skin
that folds into its own envelope?

Must each vowel therefore weigh
more than I can bear?

We loved you so. Still do.

I'm afraid if I step outside the airlock

I miss you. Sorely.

I'll only encounter the need

to backtrack rapidly one door at a time.
Or have you hovered above me

all along?

Could I have sensed that? Or

is it as though he's in a coma,
hazily aware

some letter is forthcoming?
How much loneliness did you know?

Will I only receive an echo?
Will I even receive an echo?

It's strange to inhabit days, then years
without you, to keep changing

without being able to phone.
Do you miss chatting loosely,

puncturing my big-brother certainties

after the rates went down at eleven?

If you've had leisure to float
through re-runs of our childhood dramas,

could we at least compare notes?
Do I need to press "Rewind"?

Are you forbidden to give advice?
Is he even a coherent

consciousness?
Do you watch my skin wrinkle,

my face grow more like Dad's,
my edges soften?

Or is What-He-Was
in a dimension beyond

I'm nearing the end of this page.
beyond consciousness?

Have you completely forgiven me?
Beyond what I can perceive?

How will your messages arrive?
Will I be able to decipher them?

Have you completely forgotten me?
Is no sequel possible?

What could the future mean
to the dead?

v.
Communications is plural,
implying there will be more.
Because the purpose of these
yet-to-come space-borne messages is
to foster peace. Whose peace?
Mine? His? Is he troubled?
Does what I'm sprinting down the block
to drop inside a metal box
and shake its creaky sideways door
back and forth one extra time
to make sure it's fallen
have anything to do with answers
or peace?

HAND-ME-DOWN

Of course it was blue.
Its plush heft hugged skinny me.
My frame too slight, little brother, to lift you
when you were ripped big. Before wasting. Before laid out.

That first winter I nuzzled
inside your quilted coat, longing
for your scent in its lining, a folded
note in one pocket, a condom
that could have saved you.

The next two sleety Decembers I marched clenched
shoulders into early darkness, snuggled
five-o'clock shadow into ribbed collar.

Finally, I hung your coat's tatters
inside a garment bag. Now and then I slip my arms
within the sleeves, hear myself breathe.

I NEVER WENT BACK TO YOU

i.

Thoroughbred freckles dappled your deltoids
as if you were model & classic statue in one
in the slanted, amber sunbeams
those autumn afternoons.

I marveled at your grown-up realm
where you lined the path to your bed
with stacked newspapers.
Your bathroom's blaring
fluorescence I even embraced
because it spotlit my waking dream
as I'd lather your nape, gape behind your milky back.

                    *

Before those weekends,
my undergraduate abdomen had glistened
each solitary Saturday night
in my run-down apartment in the city
where I kicked back damp sheets—
my scrubbed ears a small-town audience
held captive while the upstairs neighbor, a booted clone,
& his first trick of the weekend
pounded hard & bellowed
just above my ceiling,
making my whole being blush.

As a boy, I'd spend Lent studying Jesus' doweled feet,
the tear-drop gash in his side. The body of
Christ stuck to my tongue & stayed stuck—

as if I needed a tutor
before I could savor melting Godiva
despite the martyrs.

*

Your fingertip beguiled me
(I thought I was ugly & undeserving—
I was nineteen) on that velvety sofa
as the theme of your slideshow
drifted towards skin. Mine

pulsed for the sequel. All I ever wanted:
creamy man older man bigger man muscled man,
but what came after easing off your wire glasses
four weekends in a row
wasn't all I wanted after all.

ii.

I never went back to you—till tonight.
An idle Google search turns up a †
after your name. My mind staggers.
Then I track down your death date,
print the black & white yearbook photos
of you at twenty-one, pale & gangly,
in the back row with the Young Republicans,
your tweed jacket & the horn-rimmed glasses
sported by the other prep boys you bedded
(you bragged you bagged scores of them).
That lit-up look on your face I recall,
the kissable up-flip in your upper lip.
—Now I'm on a mission, hunt down
articles you authored, a color shot
of the modest memorial your rich
but restrained parents donated
to your alma mater, *their* online obituaries
lengthy because they were prominent

yacht- & golf-club Pilgrim-descended industrialists,
& so were you, their tersely mentioned,
previously deceased eldest scion,
the IIIrd, who spilled his seed. On me.

*

It wasn't *Love Story*.
You kept miles away from "Love
means never having to say…,"
from introducing me to the mansion,
where even if I'd possessed a Main Line pedigree,
top-drawer manners, twill from J. Press,
& never, ever alluded to sunny afternoons,
by contrast Jenny Cavalleri's fiery red dress
would have seemed a flair fit to be married.

iii. Mayflower Cemetery

because your brother didn't answer my letter

because I figured that like *my* brother
an unmarried & childless son
you'd be buried beside your parents

because at first I didn't see
your cutting-board-sized stone

because it was that day each October
when a whole generation of leaves lets go

because I now know you stopped breathing
during the first wave of our plague

because I would have held you lightly
as you threw up or coughed

would've stood like a wet boulder at your funeral
whether your kin liked it or not

because to rip back dandelions & crabgrass
& scrape with my nails broken pine needles
filling in the letters of your name,

I will kneel six feet from you
year after year.

RUNNING INTO WALTA ON THE RED LINE

Walta Borawski, 1947-1994

When this "dude" clunks onto a plastic seat
on the outbound, his blond hair nine inches long,
I notice details you would've, Walta:
wide silver band on his middle finger,
chest hair where no T-shirt tames,
strip of white sheet tied to the strap
of coconut-brown canvas bag.
Edgy boots with optional steel attached.
By the time we've taken this morsel's
measure, without a glance between us,
I'm wowed by how your hover
has moved beyond words—

gifted motor-mouth poet,
you'd stroll into a tearoom
& try to blab with pals
you'd startled on the cusp
of scoring big in late stages
of high-stakes cruising.
(Queens once called gabbing there
"setting up high tea,"
but, hon, they meant *outside* the loo.)
I recall your brow, rumpled by my scowl.
I assumed you'd iron everything out
in your diary—

       ooo, Walta!
he's getting off at Harvard.
Are you going on to Porter Square (for what
—is the afterlife past Alewife)?
No, look!—he's sauntering
down the inbound ramp, heading back
to what was your neighborhood.

Maybe he's riding back & forth
between your two stops, summoning lyrics.
Quick—interrupt! If only you could
invite him up for chatty raspberry tea—to show him
your books. How it's done.
Like you did for me.

III.

a froth where the music was starting
to leave itself for air

...

...vast field of air
for which the word *oscuro* is entry

—Susan Mitchell

PIGEON ALIGHTS

*(in memory of Roland Flint, who embraced
an ungainly alter ego named Pigeon)*

Our yoga instructor prepares us for "Pigeon" pose,
sets blocks beneath men's pelvises.
We'll need them.
We drape our weight over one splayed thigh at a time
—as if a bird would pin its own wings—
and then, oh, yes, the baritone groans announce
though we're not squashing scrotums now,
male hips have no hinge.
Mindful, we're tutored. *Breathe.*

Rows of torsos comply,
lowering our bulk against our knotted-ness
to free up but not dislocate—which is when
some remnant of him crash-lands against my psoas.
This must be happening because a trickle of tears
blends with sweat swamping my towel.
I'm reminded of his slight waddle, his potbelly.
He gets up on pink feet, shakes his tail,
bobs to where my hands meet in "Prayer," and nods.

Decades ago, in the Department's underground day-
and-night fluorescence, where English profs' offices
stretched in rows like concrete dovecotes,
my knock woke him.
Flushed and groggy, he cracked his cubby door,
bared his work-week: one snatched nap after another
through another spring term, another chorus
of splayed beaks shrieking *need need need.*
He tipped crop-milk into each brood's
constant cry—

          then flew home, where his own
scribbles peeped and scratched
inside their shells long after midnight.

Perched in his cupola, with the telescopic
lens not of a hawk but of the hunted
guarding nestlings,
he charted darkness on all sides,
transcribed constellations that reach for
a svelte swan.

I lean on my shin, stretch
towards such stumbling grace.

ST. FRANCIS IN THE SUBURBS

"Go and repair my house, which you see is falling down"
                              —voice heard by St. Francis of Assisi

i.
A neighbor's concrete bird basks
at the edge of St. Francis's palm.

The slanted November sun
straggles through branches,

makes raw material for pitiless switches
look feathery, their reddish buds

slumbering towards spring.
Half-light softens the surface

of cement into powdery felt,
reminding me of January's juncos,

those dowdy but oddly most lovely
of birds—gray fluff in noon's

wan light. How I wish they'd trust
my downy side, huddle on my work gloves.

Even this mass-produced statue
—not bought at Home Depot,

because saints aren't sold there—
placed beneath a splintered feeder

against a stockade fence warms me
somehow. I compare my neighbor's

slattern quarter-acre, the visible
mildew on her sodden Cape,

with the almost Japanese elegance
of this composition at the head

of her driveway: statue; one ordinary yew;
bird feeder, now casting a zigzag

shadow along her weathered
fence's ribs—objects unaware

they form a still-life
that inspires contemplation.

ii.
Lawn-care companies proselytize,
leafleting our cars. Drop-spreaders'

teeth grind through steroids
calibrated for bluegrass. In place of dandelions

(those streetwalking scions of Satan!),
up crop yellow signs Xing out

stick figures of children and pets.
After thorough watering, weed-control pellets

dissolve as smudges in puddles;
a quarter-mile off, the scum-ring

in Dug Pond widens, baptizing a fledgling swan.
Our fingernails uproot maple sprouts

popping through tidy mulch.
—Not to mention that most holy mission

known to America: we shock and skim, skim and shock
standing bodies of warm water popsicle-blue,

no matter what frogs, pollen, oak blooms,
pine-needles, beetles, twigs, mice fall in—

then October's leaves clatter down,
and dissipation's legion of squirrels

breaks off fornicating and littering
our patios with gnawed cones

only to pelt us with acorns, pockmark
our parked Jags. But gird your soul

against that most grievous of sins:
if ever a blade of crabgrass

appeareth in your turf, o then
woe be the curse upon your deed.

iii.
My neighbor feeds Brother Squirrel
along with the birds

with breadcrumbs—a handful of stars
spilled on bare dirt near her storm door.

I glimpse chicory-blue housedress stretch
just inside, pale arm reeling in

her yapping poodle on its short leash.
She never inches forth to pick up

Dunkin' Donuts cups flung from cars.
Brown leaves blanket litter eventually.

iv.

To drop embroidered robes.
To walk naked down the street.

To live in a cave.
To sing to the sun.

To keep a skull close,
so it can gape back over an open text.

To establish a different order,
a life arranged not to intrude.

To leave breadcrumbs for one's friends,
faithfully, and to love the beast in them

as zealously as the soul.
To be frozen in the act

of making the self
a sparrow's perch.

EDDIES

I plunge, one among
many commuters, fellow
flotsam, coursing
towards a station
from all directions,
but I find myself stalling,
staring at twigs that no longer vie
for the canopy, but point instead
to the ground.

Cramped on the platform, I turn my hooded
scruff towards the steel track
where the eager soon will surge.
Just me snuggles chest
against chain-link, wanting,
wanting to whisper
encouragement to rushes
huddled in this suburban slough.

Sparrows squabble among brittle cattails.
I wonder what slinks through these
dead stalks to pounce at night.
Did I forget that predators could lurk
in any thin remnant of
nature I might romanticize?
A dark ache follows me,
although my wounds are common,
internal, and trail no blood.

At the office, I pretend
hallways are tributaries.
I hug the edges of meanders
becoming oxbows and shy along walls
where floor wax builds up.

My latest boss wouldn't know I
favor eddies, their wayward
water whirling under
bent-over reeds—

and it isn't that I withdraw
to avoid making mistakes,
because I still blunder
when hunkered down,
but I float through: silt
spinning counterclockwise.

TREADMILL, HIGH WIRE, THRESHOLD

Treadmill: you must always
                              climb,
never pause nor peer back
for fear of falling off
only to find no
plank to hop back
on. On and on,
worn steps rise before your blistered soles,
your hypnotized eyes.
Maybe sprint if you can't spy an off-ramp—
better to become the infamous femur
that strips the boss's gears
than to march to your own collapse.

High wire: everything teeters
                              on
how keen the nerves
in your arches prove
as they sight-read
one thin cable.
No time to ponder weighty Ifs—
this is when you find yourself
reduced to wishing
you had bat claws.
Safety nets wheeled in place
deceive gawkers who gasp, but
your leg hairs know if you fall
you've lost your means.

Threshold: your heels
                              could
stray or stay
glued to glued linoleum.
Your right foot could line up with

the sill's petrified grain,
but drift no sliver past.
You could dip a big toe into maybe
azure shag rug or greener turf—
test out tickle, inch into peace.
You could pogo over, spring into
an unmapped gap or old trap.
You could step lightly, find out if
you get free or get caught.

TOOTH BY JOWL

Robert Burns' Cottage, Ayr, Scotland

No means for a barn—one roof
sheltered them all, right by.
Just past a threshold,
four steps from the hearth,
a kid goat kept butting his nanny's teats.
Even with the yearling's stall
piously mucked out,
its up-chuck soaked into straw
only a wattled wall and latch away
from bread crusts turned on a toasting fork.
Though hand-me-down boots were always
kicked off at the rag rug
due to the hover of mothering,
the scoured pot couldn't deny
it made broth from a jawbone
that yesternight framed bleats
furrowing the Burnses' sleep
from the unheated side.

Thickening noontime's soup:
leeks sliced from roots that curled
into garden dirt moments before;
shallot heart more than good enough
to mince though it was just sheathed
in a rotten layer.

EDGEMERE

Gazing out car windows,
who'd piece together Edge-
mere Diner;
Edgemere Mini
Mart; Edgemere packy;
sapling-studded Edgemere Drive-In,
its empty come-hither
marquee big enough to emblazon a double feature—
Edgemere: a sped-by place
overgrown by a straggle of parking lots
that flank auto-glass repair
shop, spare-parts store,
truck stop, *We Finance*
used-car guy. But under
the minor highway's low bridge,
the long lake's lily-pad finger still reaches—
loosestrife, least bittern—and breathes
Edgemere, just before the unmarked
turn-off through a screen of trees
to summer cottages, a maze of
grassy driveways to memories
few might guess at
or pause to name.

EMBRYO OF A SAINT

(after Tchaikovsky's Overture to The Maid of Orleans)

a yolk   ready   to start flying

<>

languid brook   misty meadow   one squat tree

its trunk swaddled   in sheaves of hay

a pail of milk   as yet unspilt

her hamlet   an hour's uphill walk

from the chestnut wood

a shepherd's fritillary

maiden playmates frolicking among midges

as if there were no Burgundians

as if gilded angels weren't waiting

to enlist an open soul

where mowers turn

away from woodland

along the edge of understanding

<>

a voice can demarcate   the border of before

<>

triple double pounding hoof-beats

converge from three directions

hometown crossroads annexed again

change her gait   lock her gaze

one *Oui*   one aim

to spur towards   faster   harder

any pauses   between each battle

coiled with lords   their honeyed cords

<>

apex   buttressed

between rose windows

to canopy   coronation

a substitute crown   located

lofted by archbishop

Jeanne's epic exhale

kept muted   her lily-livered Dauphin

stands at last   anointed as King

circled by   scarlet glass

thorn-crown   ooze-glow

a lineage   a latticed membrane

reddening clerestory

simple to shatter

<>

unsecured duchies

rear-guard   skirmishes

scouts surround sentries

beyond Compiègne's gates

petite prize   of all prizes

shocked to greet her fear within

dragged inside a tower

told to don a dress

<>

past the beginning of an ending

<>

she who hears heaven

needs not leap   a second time

from eye-pulsing height

stony butterfly   grips the sill   clings to *Non*

wafts like smoke   beyond jabbing fingers

of the wiliest inquisitor

whose stake stands steady

ready for sin

DEUX LANGUES

Mémère droned her rosary in French,
bead by decade by mystery,
good night after bad night after sad night,
whispers dripping against an invisible stone.
Is this why French feels like prayer?

In the mill-town walkup, 'Titzee
dials Cookie's number, switches back
and forth, weaving English woof
with warp *français*, stitching in *feuilles* (leaves)
missing from the maternal tree's piecework branch
for the college cousin come to tape,
college cousin thrusting clip-on mike
like a Eucharist of stainless steel.
Jelly jars wheeled into the parlor
on a white enamel cart
covered with unwrinkled tinfoil,
immaculate as an altar cloth:
"It's the least you would expect.
Aimeriez-vous quelque chose à boire?
Would you like something to drink?"

At my own baby shower, afloat, swaddled
in dream, did I hear my great-aunt's blabber
and later guess the lilt of kitchen chitchat *(placotage)*?
Later grasp the thrust of fricatives, curves of phrases—
not in my temporal lobe but in the marrow of my ribs,
where I read the downbeat of cadences,
inflected gestures of my mother
who ceased speaking *la belle langue*

when she entered America by walking to school
then raced home wailing *Maman!*?
(*École.* No: school.)

Can unschooled ears
shoot unmapped prepositions like rapids
as rainwater spills, cataract by cataract,
off a continent's brow?
Can a far-off century's patois
sound homey as a lullaby
because rivers gurgle underground
(*glouglou, glouglou*)? Was this the song beneath
"slang" heard only at home (*patates, patates*),
faint as the hint of an unvoiced consonant
barely spicing the vowel that precedes it?

In the *langue* that's mostly absent,
there's a word for one-eyed men.
There's a word for one-armed men.
It's the word for one-armed chairs.
Piquant *mots* (*poil*) without parallel
in King George's tongue. Though the border
is a river draining the same rain
(*bordure, rivière*),
though the border is a river
and carrier of all flags,
something as grudgingly translated
as a rogue hair (*poil, poil*) poking up
from Cyrano's nose
might get lost in the crossing.

When I came upon the pebbled path linking each
Station of the Cross in the garden

beside Ste. Anne de Beaupré, no nun needed to instruct
that pea-stones awaited our knees
(*the least you'd expect*).
When my heathen sweetheart
sped through side chapels only to be halted by
stained-glass stoning, upside-down crucifixion,
sun-stoked bonfire scorching a stake,
sans hesitation, I retold their martyrdoms,
my first language intact, easily taught.

;

If I banished you, I'd have one fewer pause,
                              one fewer percussive
my baton could coax in,
                    when rests and their measure-
stretched or quarter-note
                         hushes (what hangs between
raindrops and their patter) matter—
                              a more-than-comma clearing
among dank vines;
             a whitewashed frame
for a friend's first, halting phrase;
                              a blinking red light at the fork
where I turn the GPS off and decide
                    to be kind.

If I shrug and agree
             you're too fusty to be retro yet
—a stile between fields
                   in some forgotten fairy tale—
how will anyone herd lists
                    that straggle as they graze,
or latch
      a friar's acre of silence,
or convey the hover
             of an eyelash
about to kiss an ear.

IV.

as though he were an experiment in a glass, held over a flame, about to change, to darken in color or cloud

—Tennessee Williams

THERE WERE GIANTS IN THE EARTH

fourth episode of *Lost in Space,* aired Oct. 6, 1965

Doctor Robinson, the captain, didn't change
his pants till Week Four, swapping
crinkly silver spacesuit
for felt-like fabric that flaunted
his willie before my boy-
eyes that grew
wide as a priest's host.
Even when the Doctor & the dull
inseam of Major West
cowered in a cave from a giant
cyclops who uprooted a tree to poke
into their puny hiding place like a cannon
rod into a barrel, & I blushed
with a tingle of scrumptious helplessness,
the drama I focused on was the one-eyed
marvel I pictured swinging
between the captain's thighs.
Was the front of his torso
in shadow? Wait. Were his hips
out of sight for elongated seconds
till a change of scene? Drat. If he
wore *anything* underneath, it had to be
those loose boxers some daddies favor
because his pecker & each nut
seemed to sway on its own. Finally alone
at bedtime, I murmured *I firmly resolve,*
with the help of Thy grace, to sin no more
& tucked my sheet beneath my chin,
wondering what miraculous
visions next week's cliff-
hanger would bring.

NEW SCHOOL

Banished: purple pants. Dumpster-stuffed,
along with saddle shoes with two-inch heels.
Heels. When I first came upon the pair of them,
spot-lit within the Thom McAn window for men,
I stood anxious & transfixed
two Saturdays in a row, drawn to all that suede
arches suggested
upon a carpeted pedestal.
I sported them the first day
at my first high school.

Couldn't have made a more neon
mistake. Lowered my gaze to lines
dividing floor tiles. Learned
a face won't burn all the way
from Homeroom to Math class.

St. Jude, thanks for this second school,
second chance to get lost, blend in. Navy-
blue windbreaker, gray cords,
worn Keds. At home, I practice
walking like a boy, aligning each step
along parallel lines. I nest inside
a corner study-carrel, become gerbil
without squeak, scratch,
or telltale patter of scamper.

I shun other slouching misfits even if
at lunch I nibble turkey tetrazzini alone.
Too bad this new school's rules say
even Four-Eyes play sports after two o'clock.
My shins block kicks in third-team soccer.
Muddy, sagging pads almost cushion bone,
& I wonder if I'll always need a burrow.

Unnoticed underclassman
on a locker room bench, I
don't let slip a mammoth moan
when the Varsity MVP strips down (*Good God*)
to just plump cockhead, its scrolled corona—
trophy-winning mousetrap—inches
from my enormous, untamable eyes.

WHAT HERMS REVEAL

i.
Just three essentials
of each Greek patriarch
on a square column
of stone: 1) accurately
carved head with face,
beard & hair delineated;
2) that citizen's full
name chiseled across
the flat rectangle
where chest would be;
then 3) pubic patch below,
outlined or detailed
down to mustache curls,
with flaccid or turgid
shaft & sometimes unsheathed
head of phallus (knob-, scoop-, or spear-like; next to impossible,
or not
so much) & polished scrotum hang-
ing in somewhat shocking,
unabashed display.
No more. No less.

ii.
We were a gay tour group
on an Aegean cruise,
& all we talked about
were the hunks.

iii.
I'm ashamed to admit
to compulsive crotch-
watching—that I inspect
below the waist before the face,

& sometimes get caught, & blush,
or fear the man will holler
What you lookin' at, homo?
but nowadays dudes' eyes
are engrossed by their Androids,
leaving themselves
open to loitering
appraisal of exact or approximate
position, size, & shape.
Since 9/11, white-collar guys clip IDs
with headshots & names in large fonts
to their belts, where those laminated or hard
plastic labels dangle,
flap, or sway right next to
—not to put too fine a point
on it—any Visible Penis
Lines (known to connoisseurs
as VPLs), so the bare facts
about the ravenous creep I am (o, I am)
get etched into the pillar of me
as I ogle the tripod
(face, name & bulge) of data I desire.

LESSON OFF ST. CROIX

i.
Schools of peach and baize
parrotfish sneak by
as we both follow our blond captain,

our guide, through groping
orange tentacles
that sting. First he showed us how to breathe,

how to hug ourselves
to guard stamina
& warmth. A provoked patch of seafloor

blanches, unpeels
a lurking flounder.
Lurid hues announce we're submerged in

a louche element:
curious durgons,
black with sky-blue racing stripes, mob us,

ogle us right back.
With such simple strokes,
our merman tows a life preserver

in case we wear down
or freak out. Barely
surviving a gale off Bermuda,

his catamaran
punctured, he now views
caution as one component of strength.

Nervous newbies, we
dog paddle, home in
on his trim, silver shorts, mesmerized

by muscular thighs.
It's okay to gawk
since we both do. What a cad I've been.

ii.
The Caribbean
is not the pond where
we learned as boys to pinch our noses,

float like dead men, &
give ourselves over,
against instinct, to a body of

liquid. Fearing sharks,
I vowed I'd sunbathe
on board, wave to you à la Jackie O.

But, tempting fate, we're
kabobs of ape-meat.
I tread water, waiting to make sure

you're fine. Bright, childlike
delight relaxes
your jaw, the permanent frown my wrongs

scraped into your brow.
Sea turtles wing by,
their steady tranquility green

& sure as their shells.
Awed, we pause. We're just
grasping the necessary rhythm:

first: leak; then: surface—
catch our breaths, marvel
as we empty masks, & watch light bounce

in each other's eyes
once more. Our path back
seems almost routine. We spot the dark,

tooth-like boulder where
a sandy pass shines
through shadowed reef, where our anchored boat

sways, dozing beneath
a ripening sun.
Chilled tuna-wraps in hand, our captain

admits a shark cruised
away at the start.
It doesn't matter now we are back.

CARRYING CASE

Box IV E, painted collage by Jeffrey Kronsnoble

There's a partially open box where a headboard should be.

(I hesitate to lay out	the matter of this
mattress	between us.)
Striptease.	Stage curtains,
like white BVDs,	slowly pulled aside
by fingers revealed	up to second knuckle.
What's partly glimpsed	through pouch threads caught
unraveling, through proscenium	of coarse cheesecloth:
grainy naked thighs,	maybe curled tips
of hanging pubic hairs	of indeterminate
sex, the allure	of what's gauzy
and perhaps possible	lugged from town to town,
portable puppet	theater with cords, head-
board in a moving van	rattles inside me
everywhere I	go. I stall

disrobed by this painting of a box.

AFTER JUDY GRAHN

I'm not a dude
      I'm an amaryllis
I'm not a piledriver
      I'm a deltoid reader
I'm not an armored car
      I'm a disco strut
I'm not a foot-soldier
      I'm a redstart
I'm not a corporal
      I'm a cum cry
look at me as if you had never seen a fruitcake before
I'm loaded with candied ginger and explode in the mouth

SPELL'S REVERSAL

I bolt upright to sitting,
expulsed from a dream
where snickering centurions
from an absent, conquering legion
planned to rape me. Wind-swirled grit
ticked at the linen skirt
of the dais where I lay,
companioned by my pulse,
the only other sound.

On my own I guessed my instructions;
removed—even folded—tunic, loincloth;
spread myself out on captured belly and balls.
As I eyed ants scouting my slick flesh,
I prayed subservience might spare me auction
and lash. I strained to hear a camel's snort
from the direction of the soldiers' return.
Three vultures wheeled in the East.

A bruise spread across the western sky.
Its looming roused me,
evoked a fist-like NOOOOO!
thrust up by diaphragm,
knuckling past dry throat,
punching beyond my teeth.

Spurred, I rose to my knees,
staggered to strap on sandals. Even if
it would be slower, it might be safer
to shun paving stones
and cut across dunes toward grass-edged
ravines leading to the next oasis. Maybe
a sirocco would erase my path. Maybe
cavalry wouldn't bother
to track me.

But as I scuttled
I grasped it didn't matter
if elders at the closest crossroads
balked at hiding their Numidian kin,
didn't matter if scorpions stung or vipers bit,
if snarling hyenas surrounded me,
or if I died of plain thirst.
Once I stepped one step
from my spot, and didn't head back,
I was No.
I was awake before I awoke.

NOTES

The epigraphs for Section I and "In Search of Della Street" are from Katie Farris' *Boysgirls* (Grosse Pointe Farms, MI: Marick Press, 2011).

"Sand Pile with Sissy" is for Rae Crosson.

"In My Liddy Dole Sweater": Elizabeth Dole was born and raised in Salisbury, NC, and was elected as Senator from that state. She graduated from Harvard Law School and served as Secretary of Labor, Secretary of Transportation, and the American Red Cross president. She was a member of the sorority Delta Delta Delta (also known as Tri Delt). She and her husband had a home in the Watergate complex in Washington, DC.

"Interview with Phyllis Fromme": Lynnette Alice "Squeaky" Fromme has a sister in real life, but the sister here is fictional.

The epigraphs for Section II are from Andrea Cohen's poem "Segue" in *The Cartographer's Vacation* (Camano Island, WA: Owl Creek Press, 1999) and Alfred Lord Tennyson's poem "Morte d'Arthur."

"Echo": The 4-cent "Echo I 'Communications for Peace'" stamp was issued in 1960 to commemorate the world's first communication satellite, Echo I, placed in orbit by NASA earlier that year.

"Running into Walta on the Red Line": The poet Walta Borawski, author of *Sexually Dangerous Poet* and *Lingering in a Silk Shirt*, died of AIDS. The subway stops mentioned in the poem are on the Red Line in Cambridge, MA.

The epigraph for Section III is from Susan Mitchell's poem "Music" in *The Poet's Notebook: Excerpts from the Notebooks of Contemporary American Poets,* edited by Stephen Kuusisto, Deborah Tall, and David Weiss (New York: Norton, 1995).

"Tooth by Jowl" is for Margaret Hubbard.

The epigraph for Section IV is from Tennessee Williams' poem "The Interior of the Pocket" in *In the Winter of Cities* (New York: New Directions, 1964).

"After Judy Grahn": See her poem "I am not a girl," *The Work of a Common Woman: The Collected Poetry of Judy Grahn 1964-1977* (Trumansburg, NY: Crossing Press, 1978), p. 25.

ACKNOWLEDGMENTS

Grateful acknowledgment is made to the editors of the following journals, anthologies, and Web sites in which earlier versions of these poems appeared (sometimes with different titles):

Alexandria Quarterly: "Treadmill, Highwire, Threshold"

Arlington Literary Journal: "Shoot to Kill, or, You'll Be Glad You Used Glade"

Emerge: 2016 Lambda Fellows Anthology: "Sand Pile with Sissy"

Ethel: "Incubation of a Star" and "Rosemary Woodhouse"

Evening Street Review: "Interview with Phyllis Fromme"

International Poetry Review: "Deux Langues"

jdbrecords: "Pigeon in Subway"

Knocking at the Door: Poems about Approaching the Other (Long Beach, CA: Birch Bench Press, 2011): "Interview with Phyllis Fromme"

Lily Poetry Review: "My Liddy Dole Sweater" and "New School"

Mollyhouse: "Abel Has Almost No Immune System," "After Judy Grahn," and "Lesson off St. Croix"

Naugatuck River Review: "Spell's Reversal"

OVS: "St. Francis in the Suburbs" and "A Time for Us"

Poetry Porch: "Pigeon Alights"

RFD: "Running into Walta on the Red Line" and "The Woman with a Transparent Purse"

SNReview: "Eddies"

Santa Fe Writers Project Quarterly: "I Never Went Back to You"

Spank the Carp: "Edgemere"

Stonewall's Legacy: A Poetry Anthology (Long Island, NY: Local Gems Poetry Press, 2019): "New School"

Summerset Review: "There Was a Crash"

"Rosemary Woodhouse" first appeared in *The Spirit Can Crest* (Amherst Writers & Artists Press, 2003).

"I Never Went Back to You," "A Cage's Lament," and "Today, Brother, You Would Have Turned 56" were chosen as a runner-up entry for the 2021 Saints and Sinners Poetry Contest.

Thanks to Len Arzoomanian (http://www.61thriftpower.com/index2.shtml) for permission to use his photograph "Edgemere Drive-In, Shrewsbury, MA."

I would like to express heartfelt thanks to those who helped me improve these poems, including leaders and participants in Kevin McLellan's and Tom Daley's workshops in Cambridge, MA, and in workshops at the Palm Beach Poetry Festival, New England College MFA in Poetry Program, and the Lambda Literary Fellowship; the poet and teacher Nadia Colburn; and, most especially, my editor at Lily Poetry Review Books, Eileen Cleary. My husband Neil Glickman also deserves my deepest gratitude.

ABOUT THE AUTHOR

Author photo by Jamison Wexler

Steven Riel is the author of one full-length collection of poetry (*Fellow Odd Fellow*) and three chapbooks. His most recent chapbook *Postcard from P-town* was published as runner-up for the inaugural Robin Becker Chapbook Prize. His poems have appeared in several anthologies and numerous periodicals, including *The Minnesota Review* and *International Poetry Review*. He currently serves as editor-in-chief of the Franco-American literary e-journal *Résonance*.

One of Riel's poems was selected by Denise Levertov as runner-up for the Grolier Poetry Peace Prize in 1987. He was named the 2005 Robert Fraser Distinguished Visiting Poet at Bucks County Community College.

Visit his author page at www.stevenriel.com